# Healing for the Woman Who Has Been Hurt

*A Bible Study for Finding Hope, Restoration, and Wholeness in Christ*

## LENDE CLICK

*Healing for the Woman Who Has Been Hurt*

*A Bible Study for Finding Hope, Restoration, and Wholeness in Christ*



Published by **Lende Click Publishing**

Author: Dr. **Lende Click**
Cover Design: Dr. **Lende Click**
Interior Design: Dr. **Lende Click**

Printed in the United States of America

# Dedication

This book is dedicated to the woman who has wept in silence, carried sorrow in secret, and fought battles in her heart that few ever saw.

To the woman who has been wounded by life, touched by grief, marked by rejection, or wearied by pain—may these pages be a gentle reminder that you are not alone.

God has seen every tear.
He has held you through every fire.
And He is still healing, restoring, and loving you with unfailing tenderness.

Beloved daughter, this journey is for you.

*He healeth
the broken in heart,
and bindeth up
their wounds.*

*Psalm 147:3*

# Table of Contents

# Introduction

There are some hurts a woman carries quietly.

They rest deep in the heart, beneath the smile, beneath the prayers, beneath the strength she gives to everyone else. They are the tender wounds left by rejection, betrayal, disappointment, grief, harsh words, forgotten tears, and burdens too sacred to explain. Some pain is so deep that it changes the way a woman breathes, trusts, hopes, and even sees herself.

But even there, beloved one, God is near.

He is near to the tears you cried when no one saw.
Near to the ache you could not put into words.
Near to the silent places in your soul that still tremble from what you have walked through.
Near to the weary heart that has tried to stay strong for far too long.

Our Father is not distant from your pain. He is gentle with it.

He does not rush your healing.
He does not shame your tears.
He does not turn away from the places in you that still feel broken.
Instead, He comes close with tenderness, compassion, and love that never fails.

***Healing for the Woman Who Has Been Hurt*** is an invitation to rest in the presence of the One who understands your heart completely. It is for the woman who is tired of carrying hidden sorrow alone. It is for the woman who longs to feel whole again. It is for the woman who still believes God is good but needs Him to meet her in the places that still hurt.

These pages are not here to pressure you.
They are here to hold your hand and lead you gently back to the heart of God.

Here, you do not have to pretend.
You do not have to be polished.
You do not have to hide your weakness behind brave words.
You may come just as you are — tired, tender, healing, hoping, and deeply in need of His touch.

The beautiful truth is this: your pain is not invisible to Heaven.

The Lord has seen every wound.
He has counted every tear.
He has stayed with you through every dark valley, every lonely night, every moment when your heart felt too heavy to carry. And the same God who has held you in your breaking is able to restore you with His love.

He still binds up the brokenhearted.
He still brings beauty from ashes.
He still speaks peace to troubled souls.
He still restores what pain tried to steal.

So, as you begin this journey, breathe deeply, dear sister.

Let yourself slow down.
Let yourself be honest.
Let yourself be loved by God in the very places where life has wounded you.

Let His Word become a healing balm to your soul.
Let His presence reach the deepest parts of your heart.
Let hope rise again, softly and steadily, in the light of His
grace.

You are not forgotten.
You are not too broken.
You are not too wounded to be restored.
You are still held, still loved, and still being healed by the
faithful hands of God.

May these pages be a quiet place of comfort for your heart.
May they remind you that the Lord is close.
May they help you hear His gentle whisper again.
And may they lead you, one step at a time, toward healing,
restoration, and wholeness in Christ.

Welcome, precious daughter.
The heart of God is still open to you.
And healing is still possible here.

# How to Use This Bible Study

This Bible study was created to be a gentle place of healing, truth, and time with God.

As you walk through these pages, give yourself permission to slow down and let the Lord meet you right where you are. This is not about rushing. It is not about having perfect answers. It is about making room for God to speak to your heart, comfort your pain, and remind you of His unfailing love.

Each week in this study is designed to help you focus on a different area of healing. You will find Scriptures to read, truths to reflect on, questions to help you go deeper, space to journal, prayers to guide your heart, and declarations to strengthen your faith.

Here are a few simple ways to use this study:

**1. Begin with prayer.**
Before each lesson, take a quiet moment to ask the Lord to open your heart, speak through His Word, and bring healing where it is needed most.

**2. Take your time.**
You do not need to hurry through the pages. Move at a pace that allows you to truly reflect, pray, and receive from God.

**3. Be honest with the Lord.**
This study is not a place for pretending. Bring your real thoughts, real questions, real pain, and real hopes before Him. He already knows, and He welcomes you with love.

**4. Write freely.**
Use the journal sections to pour out your heart. Write your prayers, your reflections, your struggles, and the things God begins to show you along the way.

**5. Read the Scriptures slowly.**
Do not just read to finish. Read to listen. Let God's Word settle into your heart and speak life over the places that have been wounded.

**6. Return to the healing declarations often.**
Speak, them aloud if you can. Let truth become stronger than fear, shame, pain, or lies from the past.

**7. Extend yourself grace.**
Some lessons may stir deep emotions. That is alright. Healing is often tender. Be kind to yourself as God lovingly walks with you through it.

You may choose to do one lesson each week, one section each day, or move at your own personal pace. There is no pressure here. The goal is not simply to finish the study, but to let God do a real work in your heart.

My prayer is that these pages will become a sacred space between you and the Lord — a place where burdens begin to lift, truth begins to shine, and healing begins to bloom.

Beloved sister, you do not have to walk this journey alone. God is with you, and He will be faithful to carry you every step of the way.

# Week 1:

## *God Sees the Wounded Heart*

## Theme

You are not invisible to God.

## Focus Scriptures

**Psalm 34:18**
"The Lord is nigh unto them that are of a broken heart, and saveth such as are of a contrite spirit."

**Genesis 16:13**
"And she called the name of the Lord who spoke unto her: "Thou God seest me." For she said, "Have I also here looked upon Him that seeth me?""

**Psalm 147:3**
"He healeth the broken in heart, and bindeth up their wounds."

# Lesson

One of the deepest pains a woman can carry is the feeling of being unseen.

Sometimes the wound is not only what happened to you, but the silence that followed. The feeling that no one understood. No one noticed. No one truly saw how deeply it hurt. You may have kept going, kept smiling, kept serving, while carrying pain that stayed hidden in the quiet places of your heart.

But God sees what others miss.

He sees the tears you wiped away before anyone noticed. He sees the words that wounded you, the rejection that pierced you, the grief that weakened you, and the silent battles you never had the words to explain. Nothing about your pain is hidden from Him.

In Genesis 16, Hagar found herself heartbroken, rejected, and alone in the wilderness. Yet it was there, in that lonely place, that God met her. She gave Him the name **El Roi**, meaning, **"the God who sees me."** What a tender truth for every hurting heart: when others fail to see you, God never does.

He is not watching from a distance. He is near.

Psalm 34:18 reminds us that the Lord is close to the brokenhearted. He does not avoid wounded hearts. He draws near to them. He is not repelled by your tears, your questions, or your weakness. He comes close with compassion and love.

Psalm 147:3 says that He heals the broken in heart and binds up their wounds. This means your pain matters to Him. The places in you that still ache are not ignored by Heaven. God is a healer, and He is gentle with wounded places.

This week is an invitation to stop hiding your hurt from the One who already sees it fully. You do not have to minimize it. You do not have to pretend you are stronger than you feel. You can come honestly before the Lord and let Him meet you in the places that still hurt.

Dear sister, you are seen.
You are known.
You are not forgotten.
And the God who sees you is also the God who heals you.

# Reflection Questions

1.  In what areas of your life have you felt unseen or overlooked?

2.  What pain have you been carrying silently?

3.  How does it comfort your heart to know that God sees everything you have walked through?

4.  Is there a part of your heart you need to bring honestly before the Lord today?

5.  What does "God sees me" mean to you in this season?

# Journal Prompt

Write about a time when you felt deeply unseen, misunderstood, or alone. Then write a prayer to God, telling Him honestly how that experience affected your heart. Invite Him to meet you there as **the God who sees you**.

---

# Prayer

Heavenly Father,
Thank You that You are the God who sees me.
You see every hidden tear, every silent wound, and every burden I have carried in my heart.
When I feel overlooked, forgotten, or misunderstood, remind me that I am never invisible to You.
Draw near to the broken places in me and bring Your healing touch.
Help me to trust Your love, rest in Your presence, and believe that You are with me even here.
In Jesus' name, amen.

# Healing Declaration

*I am seen by God.*

*I am not forgotten.*

*The Lord is near to my broken heart.*

*He sees my pain, and He is healing me with His love.*

# Week 2:

## *Healing from Rejection*

## Theme

Rejection from people does not cancel God's love.

## Focus Scriptures

**Isaiah 49:15–16**
"Can a woman forget her sucking child, that she should not have compassion on the son of her womb? yea, they may forget, yet will I not forget thee. Behold, I have graven thee upon the palms of my hands…"

**Psalm 27:10**
"When my father and my mother forsake me, then the Lord will take me up."

**Ephesians 1:4–6**
"According as he hath chosen us in him before the foundation of the world… Having predestinated us unto the adoption of children by Jesus Christ to himself… to the praise of the glory of his grace, wherein he hath made us accepted in the beloved."

# Lesson

Rejection is one of the deepest wounds a heart can carry.

It can come through abandonment, harsh words, betrayal, being left out, being overlooked, or not being loved the way you needed. Sometimes rejection comes from strangers. Sometimes it comes from people you trusted most. And when it touches the heart deeply, it can leave behind sorrow, insecurity, fear, and the painful question, **"Why was I not enough?"**

But rejection from people does not change your value in the eyes of God.

Human rejection can make a woman feel unwanted, unseen, and unworthy. It can cause her to question her identity and doubt her place in the lives of others. Yet the truth of God's Word speaks louder than the pain of rejection. The Lord says, **"I will not forget thee."** Even if others walked away, failed you, dismissed you, or did not love you rightly, God has not forgotten you for one moment.

Isaiah 49 gives such a tender picture of God's love. Even if human love fails, His love does not. His memory of you is not weak. His care for you is not unstable. You are held close in His heart, and your life is precious to Him.

Psalm 27:10 reminds us that even when the deepest earthly relationships fail, the Lord receives us. What a healing promise. When people reject you, Heaven does not. When others turn away, God draws near. He does not push aside the wounded woman. He gathers her in love.

Ephesians 1 tells us something powerful: in Christ, you are chosen, adopted, and accepted. Rejection may have been part of your experience, but it is not your identity. You are not "the forgotten one." You are not "the unwanted one." In Christ, you are the chosen one. You are the beloved daughter of God.

This does not mean the pain was small. Rejection hurts. Sometimes it leaves tears that no one sees and scars that take time to heal. But through God's truth, those wounds do not have to define your life. The love of God can begin to untangle the lies rejection planted in your heart.

This week, let the Lord speak gently to the places in you that still ache from being rejected. Let Him remind you that your worth was never determined by who walked away, who did not choose you, or who failed to see your value. Your worth was settled at the cross.

Dear sister, people may have rejected you, but God has received you.
People may have forgotten you, but God remembers you.
People may have failed to love you well, but God loves you perfectly.

You are chosen.
You are wanted.
You are accepted in the Beloved.

# Reflection Questions

**1. In what area of your life have you experienced rejection most deeply?**

**2. What lies has rejection tried to plant in your heart about your worth or identity?**

**3. How does it minister to your heart to know that God says, "I will not forget thee"?**

**4. Have you been measuring your value by how others treated you instead of by what God says about you?**

**5. What would begin to change in your heart if you fully believed that you are chosen, accepted, and loved by God?**

# Journal Prompt

Write about a time when rejection wounded your heart. Be
honest about how it affected the way you saw yourself. Then
write what God's Word says about you: that you are chosen,
accepted, remembered, and loved. Let this be the place where
truth begins to speak louder than pain.

# Prayer

Heavenly Father,
You see every wound rejection has left in my heart.
You know the pain of being overlooked, pushed aside,
abandoned, or not loved the way I longed to be loved.
But thank You that Your love for me is faithful and
unchanging.
Thank You that You do not forget me.
Thank You that in Christ I am chosen, accepted, and deeply
loved.
Heal the places in me that still feel unwanted.
Break the lies rejection has spoken over my life.
Teach me to find my worth in You alone.
Help me rest in the truth that I belong to You.
In Jesus' name, amen.

# Healing Declaration

*I am not forgotten by God.*

*I am chosen and accepted in Christ.*

*Rejection does not define me.*

*The Lord receives me, loves me,
and calls me His own.*

# Week 3:

## *Healing from Betrayal*

## Theme

**God can heal the wounds caused by those you trusted.**

## Focus Scriptures

**Psalm 55:12–14**
"For it was not an enemy that reproached me; then I could have borne it… But it was thou, a man mine equal, my guide, and mine acquaintance. We took sweet counsel together, and walked unto the house of God in company."

**John 13:21**
"When Jesus had thus said, he was troubled in spirit, and testified, and said, Verily, verily, I say unto you, that one of you shall betray me."

**Romans 8:28**
"And we know that all things work together for good to them that love God, to them who are the called according to his purpose."

# Lesson

Betrayal wounds the heart in a way few other pains can.

It is painful to be hurt by an enemy, but betrayal cuts deeper because it comes from someone you trusted. Someone you opened your heart to. Someone you thought was safe. Betrayal can leave behind shock, grief, confusion, anger, and a deep ache that is hard to explain. It can make you question people, question yourself, and sometimes even struggle to trust again.

The pain of betrayal is real.

Psalm 55 gives voice to this kind of sorrow. David said the wound did not come from an enemy, but from someone close to him, someone he had walked with, talked with, and trusted. That kind of pain reaches deep into the soul. Many women know that pain well. They know what it feels like to be wounded by the very person they never expected would hurt them.

But even in betrayal, God sees, and God understands.

Jesus Himself was betrayed. In John 13:21, we see that He was troubled in spirit. This reminds us that betrayal is not a small thing. It grieves the heart. Even our Savior felt the sorrow of being betrayed by one who walked closely with Him. What a comfort to know that Jesus understands this pain personally. He is not distant from your wound. He knows the sting of broken trust.

Betrayal often leaves more than hurt. It can leave fear. It can cause walls to go up around the heart. It can make a woman feel unsafe, guarded, and hesitant to trust anyone again. It may also tempt her to carry bitterness, replay the wound, or keep asking why it happened.

Yet the Lord invites you to bring that pain to Him.

Healing does not mean pretending betrayal did not happen. It does not mean calling evil good. It means allowing God to enter the wound with His truth, His comfort, and His restoring love. It means choosing not to let another person's betrayal have the final say over your heart.

Romans 8:28 does not call betrayal good, but it does remind us that God is so sovereign and so faithful that even painful things can be placed into His hands. He is able to bring healing, wisdom, strength, and even redemption from what was meant to wound you deeply.

This week, let the Lord meet you in the place where trust was broken. Let Him comfort the sorrow you still carry. Let Him begin healing the part of your heart that has been afraid to open again.

Dear sister, betrayal may have hurt you, but it does not have to destroy you.
The wound was deep, but God's healing is deeper still.
The trust that was broken by man can be held safely in the hands of God.

He sees your tears.
He understands your grief.
And He is able to heal what betrayal has broken.

# Reflection Questions

1. Have you experienced betrayal, from someone you deeply trusted? How did it affect your heart?

2. What emotions has that betrayal left behind in you — grief, anger, fear, confusion, or something else?

3. How does it comfort you to know that Jesus also understood the pain of betrayal?

4. In what ways has betrayal affected your ability to trust others or feel safe?

5. What would it look like for you to place this wound into God's hands and let Him begin healing it?

# Journal Prompt

Write honestly about a betrayal that wounded your heart.
Tell God what it did to your trust, your peace, and your
emotions. Then write a prayer surrendering that pain to Him,
asking Him to heal the broken places and restore what has
been shaken within you.

# Prayer

Heavenly Father,
You know the pain of betrayal and the sorrow it leaves
behind.
You see the places in my heart where trust was broken and
where grief still lingers.
Thank You that I do not have to carry this wound alone.
Thank You that Jesus understands the pain of being betrayed.
Please heal the broken places within me.
Comfort the hurt, calm the fear, and remove the bitterness
that tries to take root.
Help me place this pain in Your hands and trust You with
what I cannot fix.
Restore my heart with Your peace and teach me to find safety
in You.
In Jesus' name, amen.

# Healing Declaration

*God sees the pain betrayal caused me.*

*Jesus understands my sorrow.*

*I will not let betrayal define my future.*

*The Lord is healing my heart and restoring my peace.*

# Week 4:

## *Healing from Shame*

## Theme

In Christ, shame is not your name.

## Focus Scriptures

**Romans 8:1**
"There is therefore now no condemnation to them which are in Christ Jesus, who walk not after the flesh, but after the Spirit."

**Isaiah 61:7**
"For your shame ye shall have double; and for confusion they shall rejoice in their portion…"

**Joel 2:25–27**
"And I will restore to you the years that the locust hath eaten… and my people shall never be ashamed."

# Lesson

Shame is a heavy burden for the heart to carry.

It whispers painful lies. It tells a woman that she is ruined, unworthy, dirty, too broken, or too far gone. Shame tries to take a wound, a failure, a sin, a painful past, or something that was done to you and turn it into your identity. It does not simply say, **"You made a mistake."** It says, **"You are the mistake."** That is why shame cuts so deeply.

But shame does not speak with the voice of God.

The enemy uses shame to keep women hiding, shrinking back, and living under the weight of what Christ came to set them free from. Shame pushes you into darkness. It tells you to cover your heart, silence your voice, and believe you are no longer worthy of love, healing, or joy. But Jesus did not come to bind you with shame. He came to heal, restore, and redeem.

Romans 8:1 gives such a beautiful promise: **"There is therefore now no condemnation to them which are in Christ Jesus."** This means that in Christ, condemnation no longer has authority over your life. The cross was enough. Jesus took sin, guilt, and disgrace upon Himself so that you would not have to live chained to them anymore.

For some women, shame comes from personal failures. For others, shame comes from what was done to them—abuse, rejection, betrayal, humiliation, or wounds they never deserved. Shame often settles into the soul after painful experiences and begins to tell lies about worth and identity.

But hear this tender truth: what happened to you is not your identity, and your worst moment is not your name.

Isaiah 61:7 is filled with hope. God promises beauty where there was shame, honor where there was confusion, and joy where there was loss. Joel 2 also reminds us that God is able to restore what has been eaten away by pain, regret, brokenness, and sorrow. He is not only able to forgive; He is able to restore.

Healing from shame begins when you agree with God's truth more than the voice of your pain. It begins when you step out of hiding and into His light. It begins when you let the Lord rename what shame tried to define.

You are not what was done to you.
You are not the failure that broke your heart.
You are not the names others placed on you.
You are not beyond grace.

In Christ, you are forgiven.
In Christ, you are covered.
In Christ, you are loved.
In Christ, you are being restored.

This week, let God touch the places in your heart that still carry humiliation, regret, guilt, or deep sorrow. Let Him silence the voice of shame and remind you who you really are.

Dear sister, shame may have followed you, but it does not own you.
Jesus has the final word over your life.
And in Him, your story can be marked not by disgrace, but by redemption.

# Reflection Questions

**1. In what areas of your life have you struggled with shame?**

**2. What lies has shame tried to make you believe about yourself?**

**3. How does Romans 8:1 speak to your heart in this season?**

**4. Are there places where you are still hiding emotionally or spiritually because of shame?**

**5. What would it mean for you to fully believe that in Christ, you are forgiven, loved, and being restored?**

# Journal Prompt

Write honestly about the shame you have carried. Where did it begin? How has it affected the way you see yourself, your relationship with God, or your ability to move forward? Then write what God's Word says about you instead. Let truth begin to replace every lie shame has spoken.

# Prayer

Heavenly Father,
You see every place in my heart where shame has taken root.
You know the pain, the regret, the humiliation, and the hidden sorrow I have carried.
Thank You that Your Word says there is no condemnation for those who are in Christ Jesus.
Thank You that shame does not have the final word over my life.
Please heal the broken places in me that still feel stained, unworthy, or too far gone.
Replace every lie with Your truth.
Help me come out of hiding and rest in Your love, mercy, and grace.
Restore what shame tried to steal and teach me to see myself through Your eyes.
In Jesus' name, amen.

# Healing Declaration

*Shame is not my name.*

*There is no condemnation for me in Christ Jesus.*

*I am forgiven, loved, and being restored by God.*

*The Lord is healing the places where shame once lived.*

# Week 5:

## *Healing from Fear and Anxiety*

## Theme

God gives peace to the heart that has been shaken.

## Focus Scriptures

**Isaiah 41:10**
"Fear thou not; for I am with thee: be not dismayed; for I am thy God: I will strengthen thee; yea, I will help thee…"

**Philippians 4:6–7**
"Be careful for nothing; but in every thing by prayer and supplication with thanksgiving let your requests be made known unto God.
And the peace of God, which passeth all understanding, shall keep your hearts and minds through Christ Jesus."

**2 Timothy 1:7**
"For God hath not given us the spirit of fear; but of power, and of love, and of a sound mind."

# Lesson

Fear and anxiety can settle into the heart after pain.

When a woman has been wounded, disappointed, betrayed, or overwhelmed, fear often follows close behind. It whispers that something bad will happen again. It tells her to stay guarded, to expect the worst, and to carry tomorrow's burdens before they even arrive. Anxiety can make the heart feel restless, the mind feels crowded, and the soul feels weary.

Sometimes fear is loud.
Sometimes it is quiet.
But either way, it is heavy.

Fear can show up in many ways. It may look like constant worry, difficulty resting, overthinking, panic, dread, sleeplessness, or feeling emotionally unsettled. It may come from past hurts, present uncertainty, or future concerns. For some women, fear grows from wounds that have not fully healed. For others, it comes from carrying too much for too long.

But fear is not the voice God wants ruling your heart.

Isaiah 41:10 is such a tender promise. God does not simply say, **"Do not fear."** He gives the reason: **"for I am with thee."** His presence is the answer to the trembling heart. When fear tries to rise, God reminds you that you are not facing life alone. He is with you, strengthening you, helping you, and holding you steady.

Philippians 4:6–7 shows us what to do with anxiety. Bring it to God. Not part of it. Not only the small worries. **Everything.** Every fear, every concern, every racing thought, every burden that keeps pressing against your heart. Prayer is where anxiety begins to loosen its grip, because it shifts the weight from your hands into God's.

And then comes this beautiful promise: **the peace of God** will guard your heart and mind through Christ Jesus.

Not just any peace.
His peace.
A peace that does not always make sense to the natural mind.
A peace that can hold you steady even when life feels uncertain.

2 Timothy 1:7 reminds us that fear does not come from God. He gives power, love, and a sound mind. Fear tries to make you feel powerless, unsettled, and unstable. But the Spirit of God produces strength, calm, and steadiness within you.

Healing from fear and anxiety does not always happen in one moment. Sometimes it is a daily surrender. Sometimes it is choosing to pray again, trust again, and breathe again. Sometimes it is reminding your soul, over and over, that God is still faithful, still present, and still in control.

This week, let the Lord meet you in the anxious places. Let Him calm the thoughts that race through your mind. Let Him touch the places where fear has made a home and fill them with His peace instead.

Dear sister, you do not have to be ruled by fear.
You do not have to carry every burden alone.
The God who sees your trembling heart is also the God who speaks peace to it.

He is with you.
He is for you.
And His peace is greater than your fear.

# Reflection Questions

1. What fears or worries have been weighing heavily on your heart in this season?

2. How has fear or anxiety affected your thoughts, emotions, or daily life?

3. What does it mean to you personally that God says, "I am with thee"?

4. Are there burdens you have been carrying that you need to fully surrender to the Lord?

5. What would it look like for you to choose prayer and trust when fear tries to take hold?

# Journal Prompt

Write honestly about the fears and anxieties you have been
carrying. What do you worry about most? What has fear
been saying to your heart? Then write a prayer giving those
burdens to God and asking Him to fill you with His peace,
strength, and sound mind.

# Prayer

Heavenly Father,
You see every fear I carry and every anxious thought that
troubles my heart.
You know the places where I feel overwhelmed, unsettled,
and weary.
Thank You that I do not have to face these things alone.
Thank You for Your promise to be with me, strengthen me,
and help me.
Please calm the storms within me and speak Your peace over
my heart and mind.
Teach me to bring every burden to You in prayer.
Replace fear with faith, anxiety with peace, and heaviness
with rest in Your presence.
Help me walk in the power, love, and sound mind You have
given me through Your Spirit.
In Jesus' name, amen.

# Healing Declaration

*God is with me, so, I will not fear.*

*I do not have to carry anxiety alone.*

*The peace of God is guarding my heart and mind.*

*The Lord is strengthening me with power, love, and a sound mind.*

# Week 6:

## *Healing from Grief and Loss*

## Theme

**God is near in sorrow and faithful in the valley.**

## Focus Scriptures

**Matthew 5:4**
"Blessed are they that mourn: for they shall be comforted."

**John 11:35**
"Jesus wept."

**Psalm 30:5**
"Weeping may endure for a night, but joy cometh in the morning."

# Lesson

Grief is one of the deepest sorrows the heart can know.

It comes when something precious has been lost. Sometimes it is the loss of a loved one. Sometimes it is the loss of a relationship, a dream, a season, a sense of safety, or the life you thought you would have. Loss leaves an ache that words often cannot fully explain. It can make the heart feel heavy, the days feel long, and the soul feel tired.

Grief is not weakness.
It is love carrying sorrow.

Many women try to be strong in grief. They keep moving, keep serving, keep showing up, while carrying heartbreak quietly inside. But grief does not disappear just because it is hidden. It needs room to breathe. It needs honesty. It needs the gentle presence of God.

Matthew 5:4 gives this tender promise: **"Blessed are they that mourn: for they shall be comforted."** What a beautiful truth. God does not overlook mourning. He does not rush you past it. He meets you there. He promises comfort to the brokenhearted soul that is grieving.

And then we see one of the shortest verses in Scripture, yet one of the most powerful: **"Jesus wept."**
Our Savior was not untouched by sorrow. He wept. He felt the weight of grief. This reminds us that tears are not a lack of faith. They are often part of love, part of loss, and part of being human. If Jesus wept, then you do not have to be ashamed of your tears.

Psalm 30:5 reminds us that while weeping may endure for a night, joy will come in the morning. This does not mean grief is small or that sorrow quickly disappears. It means grief is not the end of the story. God is still able to bring light into dark places. He is still able to carry you through the night and lead you gently toward hope again.

Grief is often not a straight path. Some days feel manageable, and other days the ache returns strongly. Some moments are filled with memories, and others are filled with silence. Healing in grief is often slow and tender. It is not about forgetting. It is about learning to let God hold you as you carry what has been lost.

This week, give yourself permission to grieve honestly before the Lord. You do not have to be strong every moment. You do not have to hide your tears. You do not have to explain your sorrow away. Let God meet you in the valley. Let Him comfort the places in you that still ache.

Dear sister, the Lord is not afraid of your sorrow.
He is close to you in it.
He sees the tears, the emptiness, the memories, and the pain that loss has left behind.

And even here, He remains faithful.

He is the God who comforts.
He is the God who stays.
And He is the God who can bring hope again, even after deep loss.

# Reflection Questions

**1. What loss or grief has touched your heart most deeply in this season?**

________________________________________

________________________________________

________________________________________

**2. How has this grief affected your heart, your thoughts, or your daily life?**

________________________________________

________________________________________

________________________________________

**3. What does it mean to you that Jesus understands sorrow and wept?**

________________________________________

________________________________________

________________________________________

**4. Have you given yourself permission to grieve honestly before God? Why or why not?**

________________________________________

________________________________________

________________________________________

**5. What would it look like for you to let God comfort you in this season of loss?**

________________________________________

________________________________________

________________________________________

# Journal Prompt

Write about the loss you are grieving. Be honest about what hurts, what you miss, and what feels heavy in your heart. Then write a prayer asking God to meet you in your sorrow, comfort your soul, and carry you gently through this season.

# Prayer

Heavenly Father,
You see the sorrow I carry and the grief that weighs on my heart.
You know the pain of what has been lost and the emptiness it has left behind.
Thank You that You are near to me in this valley.
Thank You that You are not distant from my tears.
Please comfort me with Your presence and hold me close in my sorrow.
Give me strength for each day and peace for the moments when the grief feels too heavy.
Help me trust that even in this pain, You are still with me and still faithful.
Bring hope gently back to my heart in Your time and in Your way.
In Jesus' name, amen.

# Healing Declaration

*God is near to me in my grief.*

*My tears are seen by the Lord.*

*I do not walk through sorrow alone.*

*The God of all comfort is carrying me and healing my heart.*

# Week 7:

## *Healing from Anger and Bitterness*

## Theme

God can heal the hurt beneath anger and set the heart free from bitterness.

## Focus Scriptures

**Ephesians 4:31–32**
"Let all bitterness, and wrath, and anger, and clamour, and evil speaking, be put away from you, with all malice:
And be ye kind one to another, tenderhearted, forgiving one another, even as God for Christ's sake hath forgiven you."

**Hebrews 12:15**
"Looking diligently lest any man fail of the grace of God; lest any root of bitterness springing up trouble you, and thereby many be defiled."

**Psalm 37:8**
"Cease from anger, and forsake wrath: fret not thyself in any wise to do evil."

# Lesson

Anger often grows where pain has been left untreated.

When a woman has been wounded deeply, anger can rise as
a response to injustice, betrayal, rejection, disappointment, or
prolonged hurt. Sometimes anger feels loud and obvious.
Other times it settles quietly beneath the surface and turns
into bitterness. What began as pain can slowly harden into
resentment, irritation, or a deep inner heaviness.

Anger itself is often a signal that something inside hurts.

There are times when anger rises because something wrong
was done. A wound was ignored. A heart was mishandled.
Trust was broken. Boundaries were crossed. In that sense,
anger can reveal that something painful has happened. But if
anger is not surrendered to God, it can begin to take root and
grow into bitterness.

Bitterness is dangerous because it does not stay contained.

Hebrews 12:15 warns about a **root of bitterness**. Roots grow
beneath the surface. They are not always visible at first, but
they spread quietly and affect everything around them.
Bitterness can steal peace, cloud joy, harden the heart, strain
relationships, and keep a woman emotionally tied to the very
pain she longs to be free from.

God does not want your hurt to become a prison.

Ephesians 4:31–32 lovingly calls us to put away bitterness,
wrath, and anger. This does not mean pretending the wound
did not matter. It does not mean denying what happened. It

means refusing to let pain rule your heart any longer. It means inviting God to deal with the deeper wound so anger does not become your resting place.

Sometimes bitterness feels like protection. It can seem easier to stay hard than to become tender again. But bitterness does not truly protect the heart. It poisons it. It keeps old pain alive and makes healing harder to receive. The Lord wants to free you from that burden.

Psalm 37:8 says, **"Cease from anger, and forsake wrath."** God would never ask you to lay something down without offering something better in its place. He offers peace for the heart that has been agitated. He offers healing for the wound beneath the anger. He offers grace that softens what pain has tried to harden.

Healing from anger and bitterness begins with honesty.

It begins when you stop denying the hurt and bring it before God. It begins when you say, "Lord, this wounded me, and I do not want this pain to grow into something that controls me." It begins when you let Him search your heart, expose what has taken root, and wash it with His truth, His mercy, and His peace.

Dear sister, the anger may be real, but it does not have to rule you.
The bitterness may have tried to take root, but God can uproot it.
The pain may have been deep, but His healing goes deeper still.

You do not have to stay trapped in resentment.
You do not have to carry the poison of bitterness any longer.

The Lord is able to heal the wound beneath the anger and restore tenderness to your heart.

# Reflection Questions

1. What hurt or disappointment may be feeding anger in your heart right now?

2. Have you noticed bitterness taking root in any area of your life? If so, how?

3. How has anger or resentment affected your peace, relationships, or spiritual life?

4. What do you think God wants to heal beneath your anger?

5. What would it look like for you to surrender bitterness to the Lord and ask Him to soften your heart?

# Journal Prompt

Write honestly about the anger, resentment, or bitterness you
have been carrying. What pain is underneath it? How has it
affected your heart? Then write a prayer asking God to
uproot bitterness, heal the deeper wound, and restore His
peace within you.

# Prayer

Heavenly Father,
You see the anger I have carried and the hurt beneath it.
You know the places where pain has tried to grow into
bitterness.
Thank You that I do not have to stay trapped in resentment.
Please search my heart and show me what needs to be
healed.
Uproot every root of bitterness and wash my heart with Your
peace.
Help me release wrath, anger, and resentment into Your
hands.
Soften the places in me that have grown hard through pain.
Teach me how to walk in freedom, peace, and grace again.
In Jesus' name, amen.

# Healing Declaration

*God is healing the hurt beneath my anger.*

*Bitterness will not take root in my heart.*

*The Lord is restoring peace and tenderness within me.*

*I am being set free from resentment by the grace of God.*

# Week 8:

# *Healing from Unforgiveness*

## Theme

God can help you release what hurt you and walk in freedom.

## Focus Scriptures

**Colossians 3:13**
"Forbearing one another, and forgiving one another, if any man have a quarrel against any: even as Christ forgave you, so also do ye."

**Matthew 6:14**
"For if ye forgive men their trespasses, your heavenly Father will also forgive you."

**Ephesians 4:32**
"And be ye kind one to another, tenderhearted, forgiving one another, even as God for Christ's sake hath forgiven you."

# Lesson

Unforgiveness is often the heart's way of holding on to pain.

When a woman has been deeply hurt, forgiveness can feel very hard. Sometimes the wound was so deep, so unfair, or so life-changing that the heart wants to hold on to the offense as protection. It may feel safer to keep the pain guarded than to release it. It may feel like forgiving would excuse what happened or make the wound seem small.

But forgiveness is not saying the hurt did not matter.

Forgiveness does not call evil good.
It does not erase accountability.
It does not mean trust is instantly restored.
And it does not mean the pain was small.

Forgiveness means choosing to place the offense into God's hands instead of carrying it as a lifelong burden. It is releasing your right to revenge and entrusting justice to the Lord. It is saying, "God, this hurt me deeply, but I do not want this wound to keep ruling my heart."

Unforgiveness keeps pain alive.

It ties the heart to the offense again and again. It can keep old wounds open, steal peace, and make it harder for healing to flow freely. Many women are carrying not only the original hurt, but also the heavy burden of unresolved unforgiveness. And that burden can quietly affect their thoughts, emotions, prayers, and peace.

God does not ask you to forgive because He ignores your pain. He asks you to forgive because He wants to free your heart.

Colossians 3:13 reminds us to forgive as Christ forgave us. What a humbling and holy truth. We have been shown mercy beyond what we could ever deserve. Jesus forgave us fully, lovingly, and sacrificially. Through His grace, He gives us the strength to extend forgiveness, even when it feels impossible in our own strength.

Forgiveness is often a process.

Sometimes it happens in layers. Sometimes you release the pain to God, and later you must release it again. Sometimes the wound tries to return to your mind, and you must once more surrender it to the Lord. This does not mean you failed. It means healing is unfolding.

Forgiveness is not weakness.
It is spiritual strength.
It is not pretending.
It is surrender.
It is not approval of the wrong.
It is freedom from the prison of it.

Matthew 6:14 reminds us that forgiveness matters deeply to God. A heart that receives mercy is also called to give mercy. This does not mean the journey is easy, but it does mean it is sacred. God will help you do what He is asking of you.

This week, ask the Lord to show you if there is someone you still need to forgive. It may be a person who wounded you, abandoned you, betrayed you, or spoke words that cut deeply. It may even be yourself. Bring that pain into the light of God's presence and ask Him for grace to release it.

Dear sister, forgiveness may feel costly, but so is carrying unforgiveness.
One leads to bondage.
The other leads to freedom.

You do not have to keep drinking the poison of the past.
You do not have to stay chained to the wound.
God is able to help you release what has hurt you and begin walking in freedom.

# Reflection Questions

**1. Is there someone in your life you have struggled to forgive? What made the wound so difficult to release?**

_______________________________

_______________________________

_______________________________

**2. How has unforgiveness affected your peace, your heart, or your relationship with God?**

_______________________________

_______________________________

_______________________________

**3. What fears or thoughts make forgiveness feel difficult for you?**

_______________________________

_______________________________

_______________________________

**4. How does it speak to your heart that Christ has forgiven you fully and lovingly?**

_______________________________

_______________________________

_______________________________

**5. What would it look like for you to place this hurt into God's hands and begin the journey of forgiveness?**

_______________________________

_______________________________

_______________________________

# Journal Prompt

Write honestly about a person or situation you have
struggled to forgive. Tell God how deeply it hurt and why it
has been hard to let go. Then write a prayer asking Him to
help you release the offense, trust Him with justice, and
begin walking in the freedom that forgiveness brings.

# Prayer

Heavenly Father,
You know the wounds I have carried and the pain that has
made forgiveness difficult.
You see the offenses that still ache in my heart and the places
where I have struggled to let go.
Thank You for the mercy You have shown me through Jesus
Christ.
Thank You that I have been forgiven, loved, and covered by
Your grace.
Please help me do what feels too hard in my own strength.
Give me the courage to release this hurt into Your hands.
Teach me to trust You with justice, healing, and what I
cannot fix.
Free my heart from the burden of unforgiveness and fill me
with Your peace.
In Jesus' name, amen.

# Healing Declaration

*By God's grace, I choose forgiveness.*

*I will not stay chained to the pain of the past.*

*The Lord is helping me release what hurt me.*

*Forgiveness is opening the door to healing and freedom in my heart.*

# Week 9:

# *Healing from Loneliness*

## Theme

God is with you in the lonely places and His presence is enough to hold your heart.

## Focus Scriptures

**Deuteronomy 31:6**
"Be strong and of a good courage, fear not, nor be afraid of them: for the Lord thy God, he it is that doth go with thee; he will not fail thee, nor forsake thee."

**Psalm 68:6**
"God setteth the solitary in families…"

**Isaiah 43:2**
"When thou passest through the waters, I will be with thee…"

# Lesson

Loneliness can be one of the quietest pains a woman carries.

It does not always mean there are no people around you.
Sometimes loneliness is felt most deeply even in a crowded
room, in a busy season, or in the middle of serving others. It
can come when you feel misunderstood, unsupported,
forgotten, disconnected, or unseen in the places where you
longed to feel close and loved.

Loneliness has a way of touching deep places in the heart.

It can make a woman feel as though no one truly
understands what she is carrying. It can whisper that she has
been left behind, overlooked, or set apart in a painful way.
Over time, loneliness can begin to weigh on the emotions,
drain strength, and make the heart feel weary and hollow.

But even in loneliness, you are not abandoned.

Deuteronomy 31:6 gives this strong and beautiful promise:
**"He will not fail thee, nor forsake thee."** What comfort there
is in knowing that even when people fall short, God remains
faithful. Even when others are absent, the Lord is present.
Even when your heart feels alone, you are never outside the
reach of His love.

God's presence is not a small comfort.
It is holy companionship for the lonely soul.

Isaiah 43:2 reminds us that when you pass through deep
waters, God says, **"I will be with thee."** He does not always
remove every lonely season immediately, but He promises

His presence in the middle of it. He walks with you through it. He stays with you in the places where silence feels heavy and where the heart aches for connection.

Psalm 68:6 also gives hope: **"God setteth the solitary in families."** This shows the heart of God toward the lonely. He sees the one who feels isolated. He cares about the one who feels left out. He is able to bring loving connections, spiritual family, godly companionship, and comfort in ways that only He can arrange.

Loneliness can sometimes tempt a woman to believe she does not matter, that no one sees her, or that she will always feel this way. But loneliness does not tell the truth about your worth. It does not tell the truth about God's presence. And it does not tell the truth about your future.

The Lord is with you in the lonely places.
He sees the ache no one else notices.
He knows the prayers you have whispered in silence.
He understands the longing in your heart to be known,
loved, and held close.

This week, let yourself be honest with God about the loneliness you have carried. Do not hide it. Do not minimize it. Bring that ache into His presence. Let Him comfort the solitary places in your heart and remind you that you are deeply seen and never truly alone.

Dear sister, loneliness may have visited your heart, but it does not define your life.
God has not forgotten you.
He has not left you behind.
He is with you, even here.

And the presence of God can hold you in ways no human
hand ever could.

# Reflection Questions

1. In what ways have you been experiencing loneliness in this season?

2. Have you ever felt lonely even when surrounded by other people? What did that feel like for you?

3. How does it comfort your heart to know that God promises never to leave or forsake you?

4. What lies has loneliness tried to whisper to you about your worth, your future, or your place in the lives of others?

5. What would it look like for you to let God meet you in the lonely places of your heart this week?

# Journal Prompt

Write honestly about the loneliness you have felt. Tell God where it hurts, what you long for, and how this season has affected your heart. Then write a prayer inviting Him to fill the lonely places with His presence, comfort, and peace.

# Prayer

Heavenly Father,
You see the lonely places in my heart and the ache I have carried in silence.
You know the times I have felt forgotten, misunderstood, or deeply alone.
Thank You that You promise never to leave me nor forsake me.
Thank You that Your presence is with me even in the quiet and empty places.
Please comfort my heart and remind me that I am not abandoned.
Fill the lonely places within me with Your peace, Your love, and Your nearness.
Help me rest in the truth that I am seen, known, and held by You.
And in Your perfect time, bring the right encouragement, connection, and support into my life.
In Jesus' name, amen.

# Healing Declaration

*I am not alone.*

*God is with me and He will not forsake me.*

*The Lord sees the lonely places in my heart.*

*His presence is comforting me, keeping me, and carrying me.*

# Week 10:

## *Restoring Identity in Christ*

## Theme

Your pain is real, but it is not your identity.

## Focus Scriptures

**2 Corinthians 5:17**
"Therefore if any man be in Christ, he is a new creature: old things are passed away; behold, all things are become new."

**1 Peter 2:9**
"But ye are a chosen generation, a royal priesthood, an holy nation, a peculiar people; that ye should shew forth the praises of him who hath called you out of darkness into his marvellous light."

**Ephesians 2:10**
"For we are his workmanship, created in Christ Jesus unto good works, which God hath before ordained that we should walk in them."

# Lesson

One of the deepest effects of pain is that it can begin to reshape how a woman sees herself.

After rejection, betrayal, shame, grief, fear, or loneliness, it is easy to begin identifying with the wound. Instead of seeing herself as God sees her, a woman may quietly begin to believe she is the rejected one, the broken one, the abandoned one, the forgotten one, or the woman who will never be whole again.

Pain speaks loudly.
But it does not have the right to name you.

Only God has that right.

The world may define people by their past, their failures, their wounds, or what was done to them. But in Christ, your identity is not built on what hurt you. It is built on who redeemed you. The cross has spoken something stronger over your life than pain ever could.

2 Corinthians 5:17 tells us that if anyone is in Christ, she is a new creation. That means your story does not end in the old places. It means what was broken does not have the final word. It means that through Christ, God is doing a new work in you. Your past may be part of your testimony, but it is not the prison you must live in forever.

1 Peter 2:9 is full of beauty and strength. It reminds you that you are **chosen**, **royal**, **holy**, and called by God. These are not small words. These are heaven's words over your life. When the enemy tries to label you by your wounds, God reminds

you of your true identity. You are chosen by Him. You
belong to Him. You have been called out of darkness into His
marvelous light.

Ephesians 2:10 says you are His workmanship. You are not
forgotten scraps of a ruined story. You are the careful work of
God's hands. Even in seasons when you feel weak, God has
not discarded you. He is still shaping, restoring, refining, and
lovingly forming your life according to His purpose.

Restoring identity in Christ means learning to agree with
God's truth again.

It means letting His Word become louder than the lies of
your pain.
It means refusing to wear labels that Heaven never gave you.
It means remembering that what happened to you is not the
same as who you are.

You are not your wound.
You are not your failure.
You are not your fear.
You are not your shame.
You are not what others called you in your broken moments.

In Christ, you are new.
In Christ, you are chosen.
In Christ, you are God's workmanship.
In Christ, you are deeply loved, fully seen, and being
restored.

This week, let God peel away every false label your pain has
tried to place on you. Let Him speak truth over your heart.
Let Him remind you that your identity has never been in the
wound, but in the One who heals.

Dear sister, pain may have touched your life, but it does not define your name.
Your identity is not found in what broke you.
Your identity is found in Christ.

And in Him, you are still beautiful, still chosen, and still becoming all He created you to be.

# Reflection Questions

**1. What labels has pain, rejection, or past hurt tried to place on your life?**

**2. In what ways have you struggled to see yourself the way God sees you?**

**3. Which truth from today's Scriptures speaks most deeply to your heart, and why?**

**4. What false identity do you need to lay down so you can embrace your identity in Christ?**

**5. What would begin to change if you truly believed that you are chosen, new, and God's workmanship?**

# Journal Prompt

Write honestly about the labels you have carried because of
pain, failure, rejection, or brokenness. Then write what God's
Word says about you instead. Make two lists if needed: one
for the lies you have believed, and one for the truth God
declares over your life in Christ.

# Prayer

Heavenly Father,
Thank You that my identity is not rooted in my pain, but in
Your love.
Thank You that in Christ I am a new creation.
You know every false label I have carried and every lie I have
believed about myself.
Please remove from my heart everything that does not agree
with Your truth.
Help me see myself through Your eyes.
Remind me that I am chosen, loved, and created with
purpose.
Heal the places where pain has distorted my identity.
Teach me to walk in the truth of who I am in Christ.
In Jesus' name, amen.

# Healing Declaration

*My pain is not my identity.*

*In Christ, I am a new creation.*

*I am chosen, loved, and God's workmanship.*

*The Lord is restoring my heart and renewing my identity in Him.*

# Week 10 Continued:
# *Restoring Identity in Christ*

## Deeper Reflection

When a woman has been hurt deeply, she may begin to live from the pain without even realizing it.

She may pray, serve, smile, and keep moving forward, yet deep inside still see herself through the lens of what happened to her. Pain can become a mirror. Rejection can become a voice. Shame can become a covering. Fear can become a cage. And slowly, without meaning to, a woman can begin to believe that her broken places are the truest thing about her.

But they are not.

The truest thing about you is not what wounded you.
The truest thing about you is what God has spoken over you.

If you belong to Christ, then Heaven has already declared who you are. You are not waiting for identity to be given to you by people, by approval, by success, or by the absence of pain. Your identity has already been secured in Jesus.

You are His.

That means when rejection says, **"You are unwanted,"** God says, **"You are chosen."**
When shame says, **"You are ruined,"** God says, **"You are

redeemed."
When fear says, **"You are not safe,"** God says, **"I am with you."**
When loneliness says, **"You are forgotten,"** God says, **"I will never leave thee, nor forsake thee."**

So much of healing is learning which voice to believe.

The voice of pain may be familiar, but it is not final.
The voice of your past may be loud, but it is not Lord.
The voice of God is the one that tells the truth.

And His truth is full of mercy, dignity, restoration, and hope.

Sometimes restoring identity in Christ is not one dramatic moment. Sometimes it is a daily returning. A daily choosing to believe God again. A daily laying down of old labels. A daily receiving of His truth in the very places where life has bruised the heart.

It may sound like this:

"I was rejected, but I am still chosen."
"I was wounded, but I am still loved."
"I have been broken, but I am not beyond restoration."
"My past is real, but it is not my master."
"I belong to Jesus, and that changes everything."

Dear sister, God is not merely trying to improve your self-image. He is restoring your true identity in Him.

He is reminding you that you were never just the woman who was hurt.
You are also the woman He kept.
The woman He carried.
The woman He loved through the fire.

The woman He is still healing.
The woman He still calls by name.

You are not lost in your pain.
You are being found again in His presence.

And as He restores your identity, you will begin to stand
differently.
Pray differently.
See yourself differently.
And walk differently.

Because when a woman begins to believe who she is in
Christ, the chains that once held her begin to loosen.

# Additional Reflection Questions

**1. What painful label have you carried for too long that God is asking you to lay down?**

**2. Which truth about your identity in Christ do you most need to receive today?**

**3. What voice has been loudest in your life lately: the voice of pain, the voice of fear, or the voice of God?**

**4. How would your thoughts and choices begin to change if you fully embraced your identity in Christ?**

**5. What does it mean to you personally to know that you belong to Jesus?**

# Additional Prayer

*Heavenly Father,*

Thank You that my identity is safe in You.
Thank You that people do not get the final word
over my life—You do.
Forgive me for the ways I have believed the voice of
pain more than the voice of Your truth.
Wash away every false label I have carried.
Silence every lie that has tried to define me.
Teach me to live from the truth of who I am in
Christ.
Help me walk as Your daughter—chosen, loved,
redeemed, and restored.
In Jesus' name, amen.

# Additional Healing Declaration

*I am not defined by what happened to me.*

*I am defined by the love of Christ.*

*I belong to Jesus.*

*He is restoring my identity.*
*And teaching me to walk in truth.*

# Week 11:

## *Learning to Trust God Again*

## Theme

Even after pain, God is still faithful and worthy of your trust.

## Focus Scriptures

**Proverbs 3:5–6**
"Trust in the Lord with all thine heart; and lean not unto thine own understanding.
In all thy ways acknowledge him, and he shall direct thy paths."

**Psalm 56:3**
"What time I am afraid, I will trust in thee."

**Jeremiah 17:7**
"Blessed is the man that trusteth in the Lord, and whose hope the Lord is."

# Lesson

One of the hardest things to do after being hurt is to trust again.

Pain can shake the heart deeply. After disappointment, betrayal, rejection, grief, or unanswered prayers, a woman may still love God and believe in Him, yet quietly struggle to trust Him in the same way she once did. Wounds can make the heart feel cautious. Sorrow can make faith feel tender. And sometimes the question hiding beneath the surface is this: **"Lord, can I really trust You here?"**

That is a holy and honest question.

Learning to trust God again does not mean pretending the pain did not affect you. It means bringing your wounded heart back into His presence and allowing Him to rebuild what hurt has shaken. It means choosing to believe that even when life did not unfold the way you hoped, God is still good, still wise, and still faithful.

Proverbs 3:5–6 calls us to trust in the Lord with all our heart. That kind of trust is not always easy when our understanding feels clouded by pain. Sometimes we do not understand why things happened the way they did. Sometimes we do not understand why God allowed a certain heartbreak, delay, loss, or struggle. But trust grows when we remember that God's wisdom is higher than ours, and His heart is always trustworthy, even when His ways are hard to understand.

Psalm 56:3 is such a tender verse: **"What time I am afraid, I will trust in thee."** Notice it does not say, "If I am never afraid." It says, **when** I am afraid. Trust is not the absence of fear. It is choosing to place your heart in God's hands even while fear is trying to speak.

Jeremiah 17:7 says the person who trusts in the Lord is blessed, and whose hope the Lord is. This is such a beautiful picture. Trust is not merely believing God can do something. It is resting your hope in who He is. It is anchoring your soul in His character — His goodness, His faithfulness, His mercy, and His unchanging love.

Sometimes after pain, trust must be rebuilt slowly.

It may begin with small prayers.
Small steps of obedience.
Small moments of surrender.
Small choices to believe God one day at a time.

And that is okay.

God is gentle with the heart that is learning to trust again. He does not despise your weakness. He does not shame your questions. He meets you with patience, tenderness, and truth. He knows what you have walked through, and He knows how to restore confidence in His love.

This week, bring your questions, your hesitations, and your wounded trust before the Lord. Tell Him honestly where your heart feels afraid. Ask Him to heal the places where disappointment has made you guarded. Ask Him to teach you how to trust Him again — not with forced faith, but with a heart being lovingly restored by grace.

Dear sister, God has not failed you by being slow.
He has not forgotten you by being silent.

He has not stopped loving you because the road has been hard.

He is still faithful.
He is still good.
He is still leading you.
And He is still worthy of your trust.

# Reflection Questions

**1. In what area of your life have you struggled most to trust God again?**

_______________________________________________

_______________________________________________

_______________________________________________

**2. Did pain, disappointment, loss, or delay make trust feel harder for you? How?**

_______________________________________________

_______________________________________________

_______________________________________________

**3. What fears or questions have made it difficult to fully rest in God's heart?**

_______________________________________________

_______________________________________________

_______________________________________________

**4. How does it encourage you to know that trust can grow even in weakness and fear?**

_______________________________________________

_______________________________________________

_______________________________________________

**5. What is one practical way you can begin trusting God again in this season?**

_______________________________________________

_______________________________________________

_______________________________________________

# Journal Prompt

Write honestly about where trust has been hard for you. Tell
God what disappointed you, what confused you, or what
made your heart feel guarded. Then write a prayer asking
Him to rebuild trust within you and help you rest again in
His faithfulness.

# Prayer

Heavenly Father,
You know the places in my heart where trust has been
shaken.
You see the pain, the disappointment, the questions, and the
fear I have carried.
Thank You that You are patient with me as I learn to trust
You again.
Thank You that Your faithfulness does not change, even
when my heart feels weak.
Please heal the places in me that have become guarded
through pain.
Teach me to rest in Your goodness, even when I do not
understand everything.
Help me trust Your heart, lean on Your wisdom, and follow
You one step at a time.
Restore my confidence in Your love and lead me in peace.
In Jesus' name, amen.

# Healing Declaration

*God is faithful, and I can trust Him again.*

*My pain will not keep me from God's love.*

*The Lord is rebuilding trust in my heart.*

*I will rest in His goodness, His wisdom, and His faithfulness.*

# Week 12:

## *Moving Forward in Hope and Wholeness*

## Theme

With God, your story is not over. He is leading you forward in healing, hope, and wholeness.

## Focus Scriptures

**Jeremiah 29:11**
"For I know the thoughts that I think toward you, saith the Lord, thoughts of peace, and not of evil, to give you an expected end."

**Romans 15:13**
"Now the God of hope fill you with all joy and peace in believing, that ye may abound in hope, through the power of the Holy Ghost."

**Philippians 1:6**
"Being confident of this very thing, that he which hath begun a good work in you will perform it until the day of Jesus Christ."

# Lesson

Healing is not only about what God brings you out of.
It is also about what He lovingly leads you into.

After walking through pain, grief, rejection, fear, loneliness,
and all the tender places this journey has touched, there
comes a moment when the heart begins to lift its eyes again.
Not because everything has been easy. Not because every
wound has vanished overnight. But because God has been
present in the process, and His faithfulness has been quietly
restoring what once felt broken.

Hope begins to rise again.

Wholeness does not mean you were never hurt.
It means your pain no longer owns you.
It means the broken places have been touched by the healing
hand of God.
It means you are learning to live from His truth instead of
your wounds.

Jeremiah 29:11 reminds us that God's thoughts toward you
are thoughts of peace and hope. Even when life has been
painful, God has not written a hopeless ending over your
story. His heart toward you is still good. His plans are still
filled with purpose. His love has not changed because your
season was difficult.

Romans 15:13 calls Him **the God of hope**. What a beautiful
name. Hope is not something you have to create by your own
strength. It is something God pours into the heart as you
trust Him. He fills you with joy and peace in believing. This

means hope is not rooted in perfect circumstances. It is rooted in the presence and power of God.

Philippians 1:6 gives such steady assurance: **He who began a good work in you will carry it on to completion.**
Dear sister, God is not finished with you.

He is not finished healing you.
He is not finished restoring you.
He is not finished strengthening you.
He is not finished writing your story.

There may still be tender places. There may still be moments when you feel the ache of what you have walked through. But you are not where you once were. God has been meeting you, teaching you, carrying you, and gently making you whole.

Moving forward does not mean forgetting the past.
It means no longer living chained to it.

It means stepping into a new season with faith.
It means allowing hope to breathe again.
It means believing that joy is still possible, peace is still possible, and a beautiful future with God is still possible.

Wholeness in Christ is not perfection.
It is surrender.
It is peace.
It is healing in progress.
It is a heart that has been through the fire, yet is still being held by grace.

This week, ask the Lord to help you move forward with open hands and a hopeful heart. Let Him show you that healing is not behind you only — it is also before you. Let Him remind

you that the same God who carried you through the valley is
the God who will lead you into green pastures again.

Dear sister, your story is not over.
Your tears were not wasted.
Your pain was not unseen.
Your healing is not in vain.

God is still writing redemption.
God is still breathing hope.
God is still restoring beauty.
And God is still leading you forward into wholeness.

Walk on, beloved one.
Not alone.
Not empty.
Not defeated.

But held by grace, filled with hope, and carried by the
faithful love of God.

# Reflection Questions

1. As you look back over this journey, what has God been healing in your heart?

2. In what ways do you see hope beginning to rise again in your life?

3. What does moving forward in wholeness mean to you personally in this season?

4. Are there any fears about the future that you still need to surrender to God?

5. What is one step of faith, hope, or healing you believe God is inviting you to take next?

# Journal Prompt

Write about what God has done in your heart through this journey. What has He shown you? What has He healed? What are you still trusting Him with? Then write a prayer of surrender and hope, thanking Him for bringing you this far and asking Him to continue leading you into wholeness.

# Prayer

Heavenly Father,
Thank You for walking with me through every part of this journey.
Thank You for seeing my pain, holding my heart, and gently bringing healing to the broken places within me.
Thank You that my story is not over and that Your plans for me are still filled with hope and peace.
Help me move forward with faith, even where I still feel tender.
Fill me with joy and peace as I trust in You.
Continue the good work You have begun in me.
Lead me into deeper healing, greater freedom, and lasting wholeness in Christ.
I place my future in Your loving hands.
In Jesus' name, amen.

# Healing Declaration

*My story is not over.*

*God is leading me forward in hope and wholeness.*

*He is completing the good work He began in me.*

*I am healing, growing, and being restored by the faithful love of God.*

# Closing Encouragement

*Dear sister,*

If you have made it to the end of this journey, take a moment and breathe.

You have walked through tender places.
You have faced painful truths.
You have opened your heart before God.
And that is not a small thing.

This journey may have stirred tears, memories, prayers, and deep reflections. It may have touched places in your heart that were long hidden or quietly aching. But through it all, the Lord has been with you. He has seen every page you turned, every prayer you whispered, every tear you cried, and every step you took toward healing.

And He is still with you now.

As you close this study, remember this: healing is not always loud. Sometimes it happens softly. Sometimes it comes like light breaking through slowly after a long night. Sometimes it is found in quiet surrender, in new understanding, in deepened faith, and in the gentle way your heart begins to breathe again.

Do not be discouraged if every wound does not feel fully healed yet.
Do not lose heart if some areas still feel tender.
God is still working.

The Lord never asked you to heal yourself.
He asked you to come to Him.

And every time you brought Him your pain, your questions, your fear, your grief, your shame, your loneliness, and your hope, He met you with grace. He is the faithful One who stays. He is the gentle One who restores. He is the loving Father who continues the good work He begins in His daughters.

So, move forward with courage, dear heart.

Move forward knowing that you are seen.
Move forward knowing that you are deeply loved.
Move forward knowing that your pain did not disqualify you.
Move forward knowing that God still has beautiful things ahead for you.

You are not who you were in your deepest wound.
You are not abandoned in your healing.
You are not forgotten in your becoming.

You are a daughter of God.
You are being restored.
You are being strengthened.
You are being made whole in Christ.

Let hope rise again.
Let peace take deeper root.
Let truth remain louder than every lie.
Let the love of God keep carrying you forward.

And if ever your heart grows weary again, return to His presence. Return to His Word. Return to the truth that the

One who began this healing work in you is faithful to complete it.

Dear sister, your story is still being written by the hands of a good God.

And what He writes, no pain can destroy.

Walk on in grace.
Walk on in healing.
Walk on in hope.
Walk on in wholeness.

The Lord is with you.
And He will be faithful every step of the way.

In Jesus, name, Amen.

*Being confident
of this very thing,
that He who hath begun
a good work
in you will perform it
until the Day of Jesus Christ.*

**Philippians 1:6**

# Other Books by Dr. Lende Click

**The Gift of Godly Friendship**
A Bible study for women who long for meaningful, godly connection.

**Daughters of the King**
An 8-week Bible study workbook for women growing in faith, identity, and purpose.

**Prayers of a Daughter of the King**
A devotional journey of prayer, strength, and deeper intimacy with God.

**God Is Still Writing Your Story**
A faith-filled message of hope for those learning to trust God in unfinished seasons.

**When God Carries a Woman Through the Fire**
A powerful encouragement for women walking through pain, testing, and restoration.

**A Life Redeemed**
A story of God's grace, healing, and redeeming love.

**Serving the Lord with a Willing Heart**
A 12-Week Bible Study on Faithful Service for the Lord

## Faith & Courage Children's Books

**Sammy the Shy Snail's Big Race**
A gentle story of courage, faith, and believing God can help you do hard things.

**Bella the Brave Butterfly and the Stormy Day**
A sweet story teaching children courage and trust in God
during fearful times.

**Toby the Turtle Who Trusted God**
A faith-filled story about learning to trust God one step at a
time.

**Delen's Story: Faith Like Sunshine**
An uplifting story of faith, hope, and God's light shining
through every season.


# Christian Fantasy
**The Kingdom of Everlight**
An epic faith-filled fantasy story of courage, destiny, and the
triumph of light over darkness.

# About the Author

**Dr. Lende Click** is a Christian author, counselor, and Bible teacher devoted to helping women find healing, hope, and restoration through the truth of God's Word. With a compassionate heart for the broken and a passion for pointing others to Christ, she writes messages that bring comfort to the hurting, strength to the weary, and encouragement to those longing for deeper healing.

Dr. Click is a **Licensed Professional Clinical Counselor, Licensed Clinical Pastoral Counselor, Licensed Christian Counselor**, and **Certified Temperament Counselor** through the **National Christian Counselors Association (NCCA)**. She is also **Advanced Certified in Death and Grief Therapy** and **Advanced Certified in Integrated Marriage and Family Therapy** and is a member of both the **American Association of Christian Counselors (AACC)** and the **National Christian Counselors Association (NCCA)**.

Through her books, Bible studies, counseling, and ministry, Dr. Click desires to remind women that no wound is beyond God's reach and no story is beyond His redemption. She lives in **Augusta, Georgia**, and considers it a joy and calling to share faith-filled messages of courage, healing, and God's unfailing love with readers around the world.